**A PRIMARY SOURCE
LIBRARY OF
AMERICAN CITIZENSHIP** ™

Your Governor:
State Government in Action

Owen Memorial Library
Carter Lake

Bernadette Brexel

rosen central
Primary Source ™
The Rosen Publishing Group, Inc., New York

For Beulah and Tom

Published in 2004 by The Rosen Publishing Group, Inc.
29 East 21st Street, New York, NY 10010

First Edition

Library of Congress Cataloging-in-Publication Data

Brexel, Bernadette.
Your governor: state government in action/Bernadette Brexel.—1st ed.
    p. cm.—(A primary source library of American citizenship)
Summary: Introduces the work of a governor, how a governor is elected, and what a state government does for its citizens and the nation. Includes bibliographical references and index.
ISBN 0-8239-4480-8 (library binding)
1. Governors—United States—Juvenile literature. 2. Governors—United States—Powers and duties—Juvenile literature. 3. State governments—United States—Juvenile literature.
[1. Governors. 2. State governments. 3. Occupations.]
I. Title. II. Series.
JK2447.C44 2004
352.23'213'0973—dc22

                                                                      2003013108

Manufactured in the United States of America

On the cover: (bottom left) Idaho governor Dirk Kempthorne addresses the audience at the National Governors Association 2003 winter meeting; (top right) Colorado governor William H. "Billy" Adams *(left)* greets New York governor Al Smith in 1928; (background) an 1805 letter from Secretary of State James Madison allowing state governors great authority in their state.

Photo credits: cover (background) © Library of Congress, Manuscript Division; cover (top right), pp. 13, 17 Denver Public Library, Western History Collection, Harry M. Rhoads, Call #(RH-861 or 865); cover (bottom left), pp. 7, 9, 10, 11, 14, 15, 18, 21, 22, 24, 25, 26, 27, 28, 29 © AP/Wide World Photos; p. 4 © Lee Snider/Corbis; p. 5 © Wally McNamee/Corbis; p. 12 © Bettmann/Corbis; p. 19 © Getty Images; p. 20 © Library of Congress, Prints and Photographs Division; p. 23 © Corbis.

Designer: Tahara Hasan; Editor: Charles Hofer; Photo Researcher: Peter Tomlinson

Contents

1 Your Government

A governor is the leader of a state government. The state government helps people that live in that state. This government is in charge of many things. It can create laws, or rules, that serve and protect people within the state. The state government can also build and control streets and highways, schools, and parks.

The office of governor is a very important part of the state government. The governor acts as a leader and representative of his or her state.

A governor will give many speeches to the public. The governor tells the people what he or she will do for them while in office. Here, Governor L. Douglas Wilder of Virginia gives a speech in 1990. Wilder was the nation's first elected African American governor.

The United States has two kinds of government. There is the national government, also known as the federal government. Then there are individual state governments. This is called a federal system. In a federal system, duties are shared between the two types of government. The federal government deals with matters about the entire country. A state government deals with matters within the state.

Duties of the State

A state government has many duties within the state. Some of these duties include:
- Keeping law and order
- Protecting everyone's belongings
- Making sure businesses are not breaking the law
- Controlling public education
- Building and fixing streets and highways
- Controlling parks and forests

The state government will sometimes work closely with the federal government. Here, President George W. Bush *(center)* meets with New York City mayor Rudolph Giuliani *(left)* and New York governor George Pataki. The three met in New York City a few weeks after the terrorist attacks on the World Trade Center.

2 Your Governor

Each state has a governor. The governor is the chief executive, or leader, of the state government. The governor's many duties are explained in the state constitution. The state constitution also sets important rules for the state. These rules serve and protect the people in the state. The governor makes sure these rules are followed.

Age Limits

Each state's constitution has rules about the governor. In many states, the governor must be at least 30 years old. In Illinois, the governor must be at least 25. The governor must be at least 21 in South Dakota.

At a swearing-in ceremony, the new governor must promise to serve the public to the best of his or her ability. Here, Arizona governor Jane D. Hull *(left)* is sworn in by Supreme Court justice Sandra Day O'Connor in 1999.

The governor is an elected member of government. This means that the public chooses a governor through a vote. A term is the amount of time a governor serves in office. In most states, a governor serves for four years. Many states have limits on how many terms a governor can serve in a row.

Term limits are very important. They limit the amount of time a governor can be in office. This ensures that state power will not be in the hands of one person or group for too long.

Voting is a very important part of American politics. Voting gives every citizen the right to choose his or her leaders. Here, Rob Andrews, Democratic candidate for governor of New Jersey, exits the voting booth with his two daughters.

3

Duties of the Chief

The governor has many duties. One important duty is choosing people for government jobs. The governor may also direct people in government jobs. A governor can also remove someone from a position. A governor can choose judges for the state supreme court. In most states, the state supreme court is the highest court of law in the state.

In 1924, Nellie Tayloe Ross of Wyoming was inaugurated as the nation's first female governor. Just sixteen days later, Miriam Ferguson of Texas became the nation's second female governor.

Sometimes a governor will run for president. This photo shows New York governor Al Smith *(right)* shaking hands with Colorado governor William H. "Billy" Adams. The photo was taken during the 1928 presidential campaign. Smith would go on to lose the presidential election to Herbert Hoover.

Running a state costs money. In many states, the governor prepares the state's budget. This is a plan for how money is raised and spent throughout the state. This money can be used to build and control public schools, hospitals, and forest preserves. The governor sends the budget to the legislature. This is the state's law-making body. The legislature then checks the budget.

The governor can help decide how the state's money will be spent. Here, North Carolina governor Jim Hunt *(fourth from right)* leads a groundbreaking ceremony for a new sports arena.

Kansas governor Kathleen Sebelius describes the budget for the state of Kansas. The chart shows how government money will be spent on public services such as roadways and schools.

The governor also works with the legislature on bills. A bill is a written plan for a new law. If a bill passes through the legislature, it may become a law. In many states, the governor can veto a bill. This means to stop a bill from becoming a law.

Different Governors, Different Backgrounds

Today's governors come from many different backgrounds. Of those people currently serving as governor:
- Twenty-four have law degrees
- Twenty-six worked in their state's legislature
- Eight served in the military or Coast Guard
- Nine served as a mayor
- Nine served in Congress (the nation's law-making body)
- Ten had never been elected to a government job at all

Many governors work together to ensure better quality of life for their people. Here, New York governor Franklin Roosevelt *(right)* shakes hands with Colorado governor William H. "Billy" Adams in 1932. This photo was taken during Roosevelt's successful campaign for president.

4 Life as the Governor

The governor has a duty to serve the people in his or her state. The governor acts as the spokesperson for the people. The governor tries to learn about everyone's problems and ideas. He or she then tries to help people with government services. The governor also represents the state when meeting national and international leaders.

One important part of being a governor is getting out and meeting the public. This way, the governor can learn about issues and ideas directly from the people. Here, New Jersey governor Jim McGreevey meets with people at a town meeting in Ewing, New Jersey.

The governor will represent the state while meeting with leaders from other nations. Here, New York governor George Pataki meets with interim Afghan leader Hamid Karzai in January 2002.

A governor and his or her family usually stay in a special home during a term. This home is often called the governor's mansion. Meetings and special events take place at the mansion.

The governor's normal workday involves a lot of meetings. The governor meets with voters, legislature members, and staff members. Even breakfast may involve a meeting.

While in office, the governor can live in a large house called the governor's mansion. At left is the reconstructed capitol of the Virginia Colony. It was originally built in 1705.

The governor's mansion can be a very busy place. Here Georgia governor Sonny Perdue *(right, center)* greets visitors to the mansion in January 2003.

The governor also has to keep up-to-date on important subjects. He or she must read many reports about the state. The governor's staff prepares and researches the reports. The governor may go to an event during the day or evening. There, he or she might give a speech or sign a bill.

The governor will regularly meet with staff members to discuss important issues. Here, California governor Gray Davis meets with his staff to discuss the state budget.

This illustration shows Pinckney B. S. Pinchback of Louisiana. In 1872, Pinchback became the first African American to serve as governor. Pinchback was not elected to the office of governor. Instead, he was appointed governor after Governor Henry Clay Warmoth was unable to perform his duties.

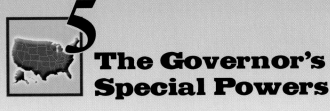

5 The Governor's Special Powers

The governor has many special powers. In many states, the governor acts as a special judge. He or she can free prisoners from jail. The governor can also lessen a prisoner's punishment. In many states, the governor is in charge of the state police and emergency forces. These forces can help during emergencies such as a major flood.

The governor has the power to call in special forces during an emergency. In 1997, Colorado governor Roy Romer *(left)* called in the National Guard to help clear roadways following a major snowstorm.

The governor has the power to release prisoners wrongly accused of a crime. This is called a pardon. Above, Marvin Anderson holds a pardon from Virginia governor Mark Warner. Anderson was freed after evidence proved he was jailed for a crime he did not commit.

Governors from around the nation get together at a special meeting twice a year. This meeting is called the National Governors Association (NGA). It takes place in winter and summer. The meeting lasts three days. Governors talk about state and national government. They talk about subjects that need attention, like taxes and education.

In 1984, Arkansas governor Bill Clinton leaves the White House after meeting with President Ronald Reagan. Clinton was attending the winter meeting of the National Governors Association.

The National Governors Association is not all business. Here, Puerto Rico governor Pedro Rossello *(left)* and Utah governor Michael Leavitt relax during a Harley Davidson motorcycle ride. The ride took place during the 1998 conference.

The governor and his or her staff have to fix many things. One problem is making sure the budget works. The number of people in a state can change each year. With more people, more money and services are needed. Services like education also have to be equal for the rich and the poor.

The governor will sometimes recruit many different people to help support his or her ideas. Here, actor Arnold Schwarzenegger *(left)* speaks about the need for increased funding for after-school programs. Seated next to him are Connecticut governor John Rowland *(center)* and Idaho governor Dirk Kempthorne.

The governor makes important decisions almost every day. These decisions can affect people of all ages. The governor has the responsibility to lead his or her state into the future. Here, Governor Linda Lingle meets with a classroom of future leaders.

Anybody can run for governor if he or she passes the state's rules. These rules include age and a few other things. Most governors have college degrees in fields such as political science, business, and education. Being a governor can lead to bigger things. Nineteen governors have gone on to become the president of the United States.

Governors Who Became President

Thomas Jefferson (Virginia)
James Monroe (Virginia)
Andrew Jackson (territorial governor of Florida)
Martin Van Buren (New York)
William Henry Harrison (territorial governor of Indiana)
John Tyler (Virginia)
James Polk (Tennessee)
Andrew Johnson (Tennessee)
Rutherford B. Hayes (Ohio)
Grover Cleveland (New York)

William McKinley (Ohio)
Theodore Roosevelt (New York)
Woodrow Wilson (New Jersey)
Calvin Coolidge (Massachusetts)
Franklin D. Roosevelt (New York)
Jimmy Carter (Georgia)
Ronald Reagan (California)
Bill Clinton (Arkansas)
George W. Bush (Texas)

Glossary

budget (BUH-jit) A plan for how money will be earned and spent.

constitution (kon-stih-TOO-shun) A written system of laws that lists the rights of the people and the powers of government.

elect (ee-LEKT) To choose someone or decide something by voting.

federal (FEH-duh-rul) Several states united under one central or middle government. Each state also has its own government and can make its own laws.

government (GUH-vern-mint) The people who rule or govern a country or state.

governor (GUH-vuh-nur) The head of a state government.

legislature (LEH-jis-lay-chur) A group of people who have the power to make or change laws for a country or state.

spokesperson (SPOHKS-per-sun) A person who speaks or acts on behalf of someone else.

term (TURM) A certain period of time.

territory (TER-uh-tor-ee) Land or waters under the control of a nation. Part of the United States that is not a state.

veto (VEE-toh) To stop a bill from becoming a law.

Web Sites

Due to the changing nature of Internet links, the Rosen Publishing Group, Inc., has developed an online list of Web sites related to the subject of this book. This site is updated regularly. Please use this link to access the list:

http://www.rosenlinks.com/pslac/yogo

Primary Source Image List

Cover (bottom left): Photo by Evan Vucci, taken February 22, 2003 in Washington, D.C.

Cover (top right): Photo by Harry M. Rhoads, taken September 23, 1928, in Denver, Colorado.

Cover (background): An 1805 letter from Secretary of State James Madison, archived in the Library of Congress, Manuscript Division, Washington, D.C.

Page 4: Photo taken by Lee Snider on March 17, 2003, in Marydell, Maryland.

Page 5: Photo of L. Douglas Wilder taken by Doug Buerlin, January 13, 1990, in Richmond, Virginia.

Page 7: Photo of New York City mayor Rudolph Giuliani, President George W. Bush, and New York governor George Pataki, taken by AP staff photographer J. Scott Applewhite in New York City, October 3, 2001.

Page 9: Photo by Roy Dabner, taken January 4, 1999, in Phoenix, Arizona.

Page 10: Photo taken by AP photographer Troy Maben in Boise, Idaho, October 24, 2002.

Page 11: Photo of New Jersey Democratic candidate for governor Rob Andrews, taken by Allen Oliver, June 3, 1997, in Haddon Heights, New Jersey.

Page 13: Photo by Harry M. Rhoads of Colorado governor William H. "Billy" Adams and New York governor Al Smith. Photo taken September 23, 1928, in Denver, Colorado.

Page 14: Photo by AP photographer Karen Tam of Governor Jim Hunt leading a groundbreaking ceremony in Raleigh, North Carolina, on July 21, 1997.

Page 15: Photo of Kansas governor Kathleen Sebelius taken by Ray Brecheisen on March 12, 2003, in Pittsburg, Kansas.

Page 17: Photo taken by Harry Mellon Rhoads of Governor Franklin D. Roosevelt visiting Denver, Colorado, on September 15, 1932.

Page 18: Photo taken by AP staff photographer Brian Branch Price of New Jersey governor Jim McGreevey on December 11, 2002, in Ewing, New Jersey.

Page 19: Photo of New York governor George Pataki and interim Afghan leader Hamid Karzai taken by Spencer Platt on January 30, 2002, in New York City.

Page 20: Photo of reconstructed capitol of Virginia Colony taken by Howard R. Hollem in April 1943, in Williamsburg, Virginia.

Page 21: Photo by AP photographer Ric Feld, taken January 12, 2003, in Atlanta, Georgia.

Page 22: Photo taken by Damian Dovarganes of California governor Gray Davis meeting with staff members on November 19, 2002, in Los Angeles, California.

Page 24: Photo of Colorado governor Roy Romer taken by Ed Andrieski on October 26, 1997, in Denver, Colorado.

Page 25: Photo taken by AP staff photographer Steve Helber of Marvin Anderson and his sister, Garnetta Bishop, in Richmond, Virginia, on August 8, 2002.

Page 26: Photo by AP staff photographer Scott Applewhite of Arkansas governor Bill Clinton, taken February 27, 1984, in Washington, D.C.

Page 27: Photo by AP staff photographer Morry Gash of Utah governor Michael Leavitt and Puerto Rico governor Pedro Rossello on August 1, 1998, in Milwaukee, Wisconsin.

Page 29: Photo of Hawaii governor Linda Lingle taken by Carol Cunningham on March 6, 2003, in Honolulu, Hawaii.

Index

About the Author

Bernadette Brexel is a journalist and author with an avid interest in political science.